The Book of Albanian Sayings

Cultural Proverbs

To

_____

From

_____

Also by author

The Alchemy of Mind, 2008, 2016
A Cup with Rumi, 2015
Peace and Conflict Resolution in Islam, 2016

The Book of Albanian Sayings

Cultural Proverbs

Edited and Translated
by
Flamur Vehapi

Copyright © 2017 Flamur Vehapi

First Published in November, 2017
by Green World Readers Ltd.
Portland, OR

All rights reserved. No part of this publication may be reproduced, stored in any retrieval system, or transmitted in any form or by any means, electronic, mechanical, photocopying, recording or otherwise without the prior permission of the author.

Written by Flamur Vehapi
Text proofread by Stella Williams
Ilir Bekteshi & Rick Williams
Typeset by author

ISBN-13:
978-1979009836
Proverbs – Albania – Kosova – Sayings – Culture

Cover photo: The Castle of Kruja
from the Museum of Kruja, Albania

DEDICATION

This book is dedicated to my
mother, who has inspired this work,
and to Suhail, of course.

CONTENTS

Map
Introduction
The Albanian People and their Language
    Family, Home and Celebrations
    The Way of Life
    Human Ability
    Work and Action
    The Divine and Matters of Religion
    Guests, Honor and Manners
    Community, Friends and Daily Interactions
    Human Nature and Greed
    Learning, Knowledge and Education
    Freedom, Country and Foe
    Hope, Health and Personal Growth
    The Power of Words and Speaking
    Money, Wealth and Influence
    Spouses, Love and Marriage
    Animals
    Social Good and Evil
    Good Qualities, Justice and Leadership
    Miscellanious
Appendices
    A: The Albanian Alphabet & Transliteration Chart
    B: Glossary of Terms
    C: Timeline of Albanian History
Acknowledgments
About the Author
References and Suggested Readings

Fig 1. Map of Albania, Kosova and the region.

INTRODUCTION

A proverb is a popular and alliterative saying that expresses a simple truth based on common sense and cultural experience. Proverbs, also known as maxims, are often metaphorical in nature and because of this, it is usually difficult to follow them, not to mention translating them from one language to another. Language itself is complex, and depending on the language (its place and time), it is loaded with subtle cultural, historical, religious, ethnic and social nuances, and such nuances have proven problematic to translate. The Albanian language, among others, is not immune to these phenomena.

It comes to no surprise to me that when I read Albanian proverbs translated into English online, most of the time I find no relation between those and the Albanian sayings that I grew up hearing both in Kosova and Albania. As far as proverbs are concerned, some linguists have translated such sayings word-for-word, completely disregarding the rich undertones of the language and the embedded cultural subtleties that come with it, and have ended up with lists of nonsensical expressions that leave the reader confounded, as happened to me while reading a book of "Albanian proverbs."

The following work is a modest collection of Albanian proverbs that takes into consideration all the important aspects mentioned above, and when possible gives the English equivalent to that proverb, in addition to the meaning of the original proverb. However, finding such equivalents for every single one of the Albanian proverbs is impossible for the obvious reason that every language carries various shades of meaning for different expressions, and also because every language is exposed to different experiences and influences through time. Simply put, no two cultures have had the exact same experiences.

The following sayings have been carefully selected, translated and cross-referenced with traditional sayings of other neighboring cultures, such as Turkish, for common themes and clarity, and it is here that one may find shared proverbs among the neighboring countries in the Balkans and the region at large; to my surprise, the similarities are staggering. This, of course, goes to show how closely people and cultures are related to each other, and as far as the Balkans is concerned, how meaningless and even absurd any ultranationalist narrative is that tries to claim superiority of one culture over another, knowing that they have borrowed from each other and continue to do so to this day.

Although limited in volume, this work consists of tens of popular Albanian sayings from several parts of Albanian populated regions[1] containing various ancient, and more recent, pieces of wisdom, advice, sarcasm, humor, and even admonition and rebuking.[2] It is my hope that you will enjoy the following selection of sayings as much as I did collecting them, and that you share them with your friends and loved ones.

* * *

Most of the proverbs included here have been collected

---

[1] These regions are those of Kosova, Albania, western Macedonia, southern Serbia, Çamëria, and others.
[2] See Janaqi (Ed), *Fjalë Të Urta Krahinore*, 2011.

from the various Albanian sources listed in the bibliography section, and a great number of them I have personally acquired and recorded during my visits to the Balkans. First, the reader will see the original proverb in Albanian, and right under it the English translation, in which I have attempted to maintain the proverb's original form, imagery and cultural nuances as much as possible.

THE ALBANIAN PEOPLE AND THEIR LANGUAGE

Legend has it that Albanians, and the Albanian language, are as old as time. According to many historical accounts, Albanians are direct descendents of ancient Illyrians and their presence in southeastern Europe, present-day Balkans specifically, has been documented for over a thousand years.[3] Although greatly deprived, neglected, and subdued through most of their historical presence in the region, the Albanians have a very rich cultural and ethnic background whether it is in language, art, beliefs, customs or traditions. This richness, however, has also suffered a great deal through the centuries and as a result much has been lost to history, like the earliest language inscriptions and various centuries-old artifacts.[4]

Nevertheless, contrary to present-day nationalist rhetoric, credit should be given where it is due considering that the neighboring peoples and cultures have had a tremendous impact on the Albanian culture (and vice-versa). The best example in point is the Ottomans due to nearly five centuries of their presence in the region. Undeniably, such long-term influence has greatly shaped not only the Balkan cultures but also those of the region at large.[5]

---

[3] See for instance Jacques, *The Albanians,* 2009; Wilkes, *The Illyrians*, 2000.
[4] See Shuteriqi, *Shkrimet Shqipe*, 1979.
[5] See for instance Inalcik, *The Ottoman Empire*, 2001; Itzkowitz,

Today, the estimated Albanian population is 7 to 10 million worldwide, with most Albanians living in Albania (over 2 million), Kosova (well over 1.7 million), Macedonia (half a million), Turkey (half a million), Greece, Montenegro, southern Serbia, and other countries of the diaspora. Albanians themselves are well-known for their deep connection to their cultural heritage, no matter thier whereabouts or circumstances. During WWII, for instance, many of those who gave shelter to the persecuted Jews risked or even gave up their lives in order to protect their guests, a people they did not even know prior to the war.[6] They did these heroic acts not for personal gains or fame, but in order to live up to their own traditions, religious and customary laws.

The word for the Albanian language in Albanian is *shqip*, and for Albania is *Shqipëria*, and the people are called *shqipëtar*, with *shqipe* (eagle) being the root-word. The Albanian language itself belongs to the extensive family of the Indo-European languages. As far as the written language is concerned, through the centuries Albanians have used the Greek, Arabic and Latin scripts. Albanian, as we know it today, is composed of two main dialects: *Gegë* in the north, and *Tosk* in the south, regions divided by the Shkumbin river in present-day Albania. The modern literary Albanian is now mostly based on the Tosk dialect. Again, due to outside impacts on the Albanian language, one cannot help but notice Turkish, Greek, Slavic, as well as Arabic and Persian words in both the spoken and written standard language.

No matter its origins, history, or external influences,

Ottoman Empire And Islamic Tradition, 1980.
[6] See Sarner, *Rescue in Albania*, 1997.

what is important here is that through time the Albanian language has played a powerful role in the development of Albanian identity and global perception, and up to this time it continues to do so whether Albanian communities reside in Sarandë, southern Albania, Bursa, western Turkey, or the Bronx in New York. Through this modest collection, I have endeavored to give the reader a glimpse of that cultural tradition of Albanian identity and expression.

Family, Home and Celebrations

Babë e nënë askush nuk të bëhet.
No one can replace your own parents.

Ai që nuk e do babanë dhe nënën, ai nuk e don askënd.
He who does not love his parents does not love anyone.

Babanë e mirë nderoje, babanë e keq duroje.
Honor the good parent; be patient with the bad one.

Babai që le djalin e mirë pas, nuk vdes.
The father who leaves behind good offspring does not die.

Asnjë shtëpi nuk të kënaq si e jotja.
No home is like your own home.[7]

Sikush është mbret në shtëpinë e vet.
Everyone is a king in their own home.[8]

Dy zotëri shtëpie me një qati nuk shkojnë?
There cannot be two heads of household under one roof.[9]

Kali me shumë zotër ngordhë nga uria.
The horse with many masters will die of hunger.[10]

---

[7] "There are no places like home" or "Home sweet home."
[8] "A man's home is his castle."
[9] "Too many cooks spoil the broth."
[10] See footnote 9.

Nuk mbahet shtëpia me miell hua.
You cannot run a household with borrowed flour.

Dasëm pa mish nuk ka.
There is no wedding without meat (served).

Çfarë ka shtëpia tregon fëmia.
What goes on at home the kids will tell you.

Edhe sytë të t'i nxjerr evladi, prap e don.
One will love his offspring, even if they pluck out his eyes.

Ec e bridh ngado, por shtëpinë mos e harro.
Go wherever you desire, but never forget your own home.

The Way of Life

Çka të mbjellësh do të korrësh.
You will harvest what you planted.[11]

Çfarë të kërkosh atë do t'a gjeshë.
You will find what you seek.[12]

Pema njihet prej furtave të saj.
A tree is known by its fruit.

S'ka trëndafil pa gjëmba.
There is no rose without a thorn.

Kush ka rënë në djep do bie edhe në varr.
Whoever has been put in the cradle will also be put in the grave.

Jeta e njerëzve është si një qiri.
A person's life is like a candle.[13]

Hallet nuk mbarohen por vetëm ndrrohen.
Afflictions never end; they only change forms.

Kur grinden qenët, ujku ha dhenët.
When dogs are (busy) fighting, the wolf eats the sheep.[14]

---

[11] "As you sow so shall you reap."
[12] I.e. be careful what you wish for because you just might get it.
[13] I.e. it burns and goes quickly.
[14] I.e. the guardian dogs of the sheep. "When the cat is away the mice will play."

Mos luaj me gurë po e pate shtëpinë me xhama.
Do not throw stones if your house is made of glass.[15]

Hajdutët e vegjël varen, ndërsa të mëdhenjtë arratisen.
Little thieves are hanged, but the big ones escape.

Ai që ngutet, çdoherë vonohet.
He who is in a hurry is always late.

Gojën mbylle, sytë mbaj hapur.
Keep your mouth shut, but not your eyes.

Pika pika mbushet kova.
Drop by drop the bucket is filled.[16]

Matë tre herë, prit një herë.
Measure thrice, cut once.

Nuk ka shtëpi pa derë.
There is no house without a door.[17]

Nuk lyhet (nuk fëlliqet) dielli me baltë.
The sun cannot be covered with mud.[18]

Bota është helm e mjaltë e përzier.
This life is a mixture of poison and honey.[19]

---

[15] I.e. don't be too critical of others if you yourself have similar shortcomings.
[16] "Slow and steady wins the race."
[17] I.e. there is an opening (solution) to every problem.
[18] I.e. the truth is clear and it cannot be obscured.
[19] I.e. it has the good and the bad.

Me një lule nuk qelë pranvera.
One flower does not bring Spring.[20]

Durimi të çon në rrugë të mirë.
Patience will lead you to a good path.

Dy herë njeriu është fëmijë: herën e parë kur lind dhe herën e dytë kur plaket.
A person is a child twice: once when he is born and once when he is old.

Siç kemi lindur edhe do vdesim.
As we are born so shall we die.

---

[20] "One swallow doesn't make a summer."

Human Ability

Njeru nuk e njeh veten kurrë.
A person never fully knows his own self.

Njeriu është më i fortë se guri.
People are stronger than stones.[21]

Çfarë nuk sheh syri e sheh mendja.
The mind can see what the eye cannot.[22]

Edhe gishtërinjët nuk jan të krijuar njësoj, le më njerëzit.
Our own fingers are not created the same, not to mention human beings.[23]

Me njoftë veten është urti, me qeverisë veten është trimëri.
To know yourself is wise, to master yourself is courage.

Budallai s'ka frikë.
Fearless is (only) the fool.

Nganjëherë edhe frika është trimëri.
At times even flight is valor.

Nuk sheh syri por sheh mendja.
It is not the eye that sees, it is the mind.[24]

---

[21] I.e. they can withstand any kind of adversity.
[22] I.e. human imagination is incredible.
[23] I.e. every person is different and unique in their own way.
[24] I.e. you might look for something but won't be able to see it if your attention is divided.

Njeriu plaket, zemra nuk plaket.
A person gets old, but the heart does not.

Mendja bënë kalanë, mendja bënë hatanë.
The (same) mind can create castles and cause grand scandals.[25]

Nuk të bënë të madh mosha por mendja.
It is your mind that makes you great, not your age.

I buti thyen të fortin.
The gentle person overcomes the strong.

Askush nuk mund të i shërbejë dy zotërinj.
No one can serve two masters.

Edhe diell të bëhesh, të gjithë nuk i ngroh dot.
Even if you become the sun, you will not be able to warm everyone.[26]

Lufta provon trimin, zemërimi të diturin, dhe fatkeqësia shokun.
War tests the brave, sadness the knowledgeable, and misfortune the friend.

Qingji i urtë i thith dy nëna.
The kind lamb suckles from two mothers.[27]

Edhe durimi ka një kufi.
Even patience has its limits.

---

[25] I.e. it has the ability for good and evil. By castles here is meant great things or greatness.
[26] I.e. you can never please everyone.
[27] "The meek shall inherit the earth."

E lehtë është barra në shpinë të huaj.
Light is the load on someone else's back.

Shtrij këmbët sa ke jorganin.
Stretch your feet no further than your blanket will reach.[28]

Ka shumë kunguj në një sqetull.
He has too many squashes under his arm.[29]

Kush nxiton, gabon.
He who hastes makes mistakes.[30]

Bashkimi bën fuqinë.
Power comes from unity.[31]

Përtacia është nëna e shumë të këqijave.
Laziness is the mother of many evils.

---

[28] "Stretch your arms no further than your sleeve will reach."
[29] "He has too many irons in the fire."
[30] "Haste makes waste."
[31] "Many hands make light work."

Work and Action

Pak fjalë e shumë punë.
Speak less and do more.

Ata që punojnë hanë.
Only those who work will eat.

Puna është shëndet.
Work is good health.[32]

Dita pa punë, nata pa gjumë.
A day without work (leads to) a night without sleep.

Po u ngope me gjumë, nuk u ngope me bukë.
If you are getting enough sleep, you will not get enough to eat.[33]

Ai që nuk punon merret me punë të këqija.
He who does not work occupies himself with wicked matters.

Fjala pa punë, si peshku pa lumë.
A word without action is like fish without water.

Buka prej qielli s'vjen.
Food does not fall from the sky.[34]

---

[32] I.e. it keeps a person in shape and healthy.
[33] I.e. he who spends his time sleeping is missing out on work.
[34] I.e. you have to work for it.

Ustau çatinë e vet e le të pikojë.
The roofer's roof has a leak.[35]

Fillimi i mbarë është gjysma e punës.
A matter well begun is half done.

Punën e sotme mos e lër për nesër.
Do not leave today's work for tomorrow.[36]

Kush flet shumë bënë punë pak.
He who talks much does the least of work.[37]

Kur s'ke punë luaj derën.
When you have nothing to do, wiggle the door.[38]

Kush nuk punon nuk ka.
He who does not work does not have.[39]

Gur gur bëhet mur.
Stone by stone the wall is built.[40]

S'bartet uji me shportë.
Water cannot be carried in a basket.[41]

Ai që ndërton me djersë, mbron me gjak.
He who builds (something) with his sweat will protect it with his blood.

---
[35] "The shoemaker's son goes barefoot."
[36] "Never put off till tomorrow what can be done today."
[37] I.e. talkers are not doers.
[38] I.e. do not stay idle.
[39] "No pain, no gain."
[40] "Rome wasn't built in one day."
[41] I.e. prepare adequtely for a task.

Nuk mund të përgatitësh një omlet pa thyer vezët.
You cannot make an omelet without breaking the eggs.[42]

Shtëpia niset nga themeli jo nga kulmi.
You start building a house from the foundation up, not roof down.[43]

---

[42] "If you cannot stand the heat, get out of the kitchen."
[43] "Don't put the cart before the horse."

The Divine and Matters of Religion

Si ka thënë Zoti bëhet.
All will be as God wills.

Asgjë nuk e ndalon atë që Zoti ka shkruar.
Nothing can stop what God has decreed.

Zoti vonon, po nuk harron.
God may delay [a matter], but does not forget it.

Të gjithë janë të barabart para Zotit.
All are equal before God.

Bëje të mirën e hidhe në det, në mos e ditë peshku, e di Zoti vet.
Do a good deed and throw it on the sea; if the fish does not know about it, God will.[44]

Kur i bënë mirë të varfrit, zëre se i ke dhënë borxh Zotit.
When you help the needy, you have given God a loan.

Kur pi ujë, kujto burimin.
When you drink water, remember the source.[45]

Kush më vonë e kush më herët, të gjithë këtë rrugë kemi për ta marr.
Some now and some later, we are all headed toward the same destination.[46]

---

[44] I.e. do a good deed and do not expect recognition for it.
[45] I.e. give thanks to God.
[46] I.e. death.

Mos përziej hallallin me haramin.
Never mix what is *halal* with that which is *haram*.[47]

Më mirë të shqyesh gojën se sa të hash haram.
Better to tear your own mouth than to eat *haram*.[48]

Pa Ramazan nuk ka Bajram.
Without Ramadan there is no Eid.[49]

Bëj çka të bësh por mendo fundin.
Do whatever you do, but always remember the end.[50]

---

[47] I.e. don't sully good deeds with bad ones. *Halal* (Alb. *hallall*) and *haram* are Arabic terms which stand for "permitted" and "forbidden."
[48] Meaning that which is not permitted in a religious sense.
[49] I.e. there is no Eid celebration without fasting during Ramadan. Eid is the Islamic celebration after the month of fasting. There is also Eid of sacrifice that takes place right after the Muslim pilgrimage to Makkah.
[50] I.e. do the right thing because death may overtake you with that last deed (good or bad).

Guests, Honor and Manners

Shtëpia e shqiptarit është në shërbim të Zotit dhe udhëtarit.
The Albanian home is at the service of God and traveler.

Buka nuk hahet vetëm.
Food is not eaten alone.[51]

Bukë e kripë e zemër.
Bread and salt and a warm heart.[52]

Kur të vjen nevojtari në derë, po s'pate gjë, jepi një gotë ujë.
When a needy person shows up at your door, if you have nothing at least give him a cup of water.

Sofrën shtroje edhe me bukë e krip.
Set the table even if all you have is bread and salt.[53]

Më mirë i vdekur se besëshkelës.
Better to be a deadman than a trucebreaker.

Më mirë të shkojë koka se fytyra.
Better to lose your head than lose face.[54]

Nderi nuk blihet me para.
Honor is not bought.[55]

---

[51] I.e. invite others/share.
[52] "Cold hands, warm heart."
[53] I.e. host and serve the guest even if you do not have much.
[54] "Death before dishonor."
[55] I.e. it is earned.

Nuk ka të huaj në Shqipëri, të gjithë janë musafir.
There are no foreigners in Albania, there are only guests.

Miku i mikut tim është dhe miku im.
The friend of my friend is also my friend.

Lum ai që vdes me nderë.
Blessed is he who dies with honor.

Miku, natën e parë është flori, natën e dytë bakër, natën e tretë teneqe.
A friend on the first night is gold, on the second night copper, and on the third night he is tin.[56]

Sjellja e zbukuron njeriun.
Good manners beautifies a person.

Ai që di më së shumti flet më së paku.
He who knows most speaks the least.[57]

As me miq e as me armiq, gojën mos e fëlliq.
Whether speaking to friends or enemies, do not dirty your mouth.[58]

E shara është arma e të dobëtit.
Cursing is the weapon of the lowly.

Kur nxjerr sekretin e shokut je i pabesë, kur nxjerr sekretin tënd je budalla.
When you expose a friend's secret, you are treacherous;

---

[56] "Guests, like fish, begin to smell after three days."
[57] "Silence is a virtue."
[58] I.e. with foul language.

when you expose your own secret, you are a fool.

Të mirën nëse e hedh prapa, e gjen përpara.
A good deed thrown away will be found ahead of you [in the future].[59]

Ku s'të thërresin, mos shko; ku s'të pyesin, mos kuvendo.
If not invited, do not go; if not asked, do not talk.

Fol për ujkun e ujku pas dere.
Speak of the wolf and he is behind the door.[60]

Shqiptari veten e jep e shokun nuk e jep.
The Albanian gives up his life but not his friend.

Sipas vendit dhe kuvendi.
Do as the land calls.[61]

Më mirë heqkeqës se grabitës.
Better a struggling pauper than a thief.

Nderi është si gypi i kandilit, po u thye nuk ngjitet më.
Honor is like the candle's wick hole: if it breaks it cannot be fixed.

Mos u bëj plak në shtëpinë e botës.
Do not become an elder in someone else's house.[62]

---

[59] I.e. good done to someone never goes in vain, even if they forget it.
[60] "Speak of the devil and he will appear."
[61] "When in Rome do as the Romans do."
[62] "Do not meddle in the affairs of others."

Ku di derri ç'është nderi.
What does a pig know about honor?![63]

Më mirë një mahallë pa bukë se një foshnje pa gji.
Better a hungry neighborhood than a hungry baby.

Dy të rrahura të bëjnë dëm, por jo dy të ngrëna.
Two beatings will cause you harm, not two eatings.[64]

---

[63] "What can you expect from a pig but a grunt?"
[64] The expression is used by the host to encourage the guest to eat with them.

Community, Friends and Daily Interactions

Njeru njihet sipas shoqërisë që ai ka.
A person is known by the company they keep.

Më thuaj çfarë shokë ke, të të them se cili je.
Show me your friends and I will tell you who you are.

Miku i mirë njihet në kohë të vështira.
The good friend is known during times of hardship.[65]

Më mirë një mik (besnik), se një çiflig.
Better to have a faithful friend than an entire farmland.

Njeriun shoqëria e ngrit, shoqëria e rrëzon.
A person can either gain his (high) status through his friends or his downfall.

Kur nuk të do një lagje, fajin kërkoje te vetja.
When the whole neighborhood dislikes you, you have only yourself to blame.

Po të kërkosh shokë pa të meta, mbetesh pa shokë.
If you seek the perfect friend, you will end up with no friends at all.

Mos rri me të keqin se të bën si vetja.
Do not keep the company of bad people, they will make you the way they are.

Mali me mal nuk takohet, njeriu me njeriun takohet.
Mountains never meet each other, but a man meets

---

[65] "A good friend in need is a good friend indeed."

another.[66]

Ai që është shok me të gjithë, nuk është shok me asnjë.
He who is friends with everyone is the friend of no one.

Kij drojën atij të qetit.
Who you should be aware of is the quiet person.

Dhëmbi kafshon shpesh gjuhën, megjithatë ata mbeten miq.
The tooth often bites the tongue, yet they remain friends.[67]

Mos i beso gjithkujt.
Do not believe everyone.[68]

Çfarë sheh në fqi, prite në shtëpi.
What you see in the neighborhood, expect to see it in your own house.[69]

Në fshatin e të marrëve i urti është i çmëndur.
In the village of fools, the wise is crazy.

Mos i fut hundët në punët e të tjerëve.
Don't put your nose in other people's business.[70]

---

[66] "A mountain never meets a mountain, but a man meets a man."
[67] I.e. people have their shortcomings, so be forgiving of others.
[68] "Hear the other side and believe little."
[69] I.e. what happens to the neighbors can happen to you as well.
[70] "Don't stick your nose where it does not belong."

Shtëpinë shite, shokun mbaje.
Sell the house but keep the neighbor.[71]

Miq të rinj zë sa të duash po të vjetrit mos i harro.
Make as many new friends as you want, but never forget the old ones.[72]

Njeriu pa miq është gjysmë njeriu.
A person without friends is incomplete.

Shoku, sa duhet aq qortohet.
A friend is admonished as much as he is loved.

Atë që nuk e pëlqen për vete mos i mendo tjetrit.
Do not wish for others that which you do not wish upon yourself.

---

[71] I.e. do not forget/abandon a good neighbor/friend.
[72] "Make new friends but keep the old, one is silver and the other gold."

Human Nature and Greed

Zakonet e vjetra veshtirë se harrohen.
Old habits are rarely forgotten.[73]

Pula e tjetrit duket më e majme.
The other's hen always looks fatter.[74]

Më i madh është syri se barku.
The eye is bigger than the stomach.[75]

Kur s'e ke një gjë, atëhere ia di kimetin.
You appreciate a thing when you do not have it (anymore).[76]

Barkploti nuk ia di hallin barkboshi.
The one who is full doesn't understand the hungry.

Për çdo sy ka bukuri.
There is beauty for every eye.[77]

Hakmarrja gëzon vetëm shpirtkëqinjët.
Revenge satisfies only the evil-spirited.

Ajo që nuk vjen nga zemra, nuk hyn dot në zemër.
That which does not come from the heart will not enter the heart.

---

[73] "Old habit die hard."
[74] "The grass is always greener on the other side."
[75] I.e. it always wants more.
[76] "Absence makes the heart grow fonder."
[77] "Beauty is in the eye of the beholder."

Me dy lugë nuk hahet.
You cannot eat with two spoons.[78]

Ai që vjedh një vezë, vjedh edhe një buall.
He who steals an egg will also steal a buffalo.

Njeriu mëson te flasë shumë shpejt, ndërsa të heshtë shumë vonë.
Man is quick to learn speaking, but slow to learn silence.

Ai që lakmon më shumë, është gjithmonë i varfër.
He who wants more is always poor.

Vetëm budallai është i kënaqur gjithmonë nga vetja.
Only the fool is satisfied with himself.

Ujku vendin e ndërron po zakonin nuk e harron.
A wolf may change its habitat but never its habits.[79]

Me i dhënë gishtin ta merr dorën.
Give him your finger and he will take your hand.[80]

Ai që premton shumë, bën pak.
He who promises a lot does little.

Heshtja është e hidhur, por frutin e ka të ëmbël.
Silence is distasteful, but its fruit is sweet.

Ai që di të bëj lajka, di dhe të shpifë.
He who knows how to flatter also knows how to

---

[78] "You can't be in two places at once."
[79] I.e. one always goes back to one's old ways: "A leopard cannot change its spots."
[80] "Give someone an inch and he will take a mile."

slander.[81]

Molla bie nën mollë.
The apple falls under the apple tree.[82]

Të gjithë derrat një fytyrë kanë.
All pigs look alike.

Peshku i madh e ha të voglin.
Big fish devour small fish.

Pas lufte të gjithë bëhen trima.
After the war all become brave.

Peshku në det, tigani në zjarr.
The fish in the sea, and the frying pan already over the fire.[83]

E dogji qumështi, i fryen kosit.
He got burned by the [hot] milk and now blows on the yogurt.[84]

S'ka njeri pa një të keqe.
There are no flawless people.

---

[81] I.e. will lie and cheat.
[82] "The apple doesn't fall far from the tree."
[83] "Don't count the chickens before they are hatched" or "Don't put the cart before the horse."
[84] "Once bitten twice shy."

Learning, Knowledge and Education

Dituria nuk falet, por fitohet.
Knowledge is not given, it is gained.

Dija është dritë, padija terr.
Knowledge is light, ignorance is darkness.

Dituria s'ka kufi.
There is no end to knowledge.

Shkolla të hap sytë.
Education will open your eyes.

Cdo hap drejt kulturës, është hap drejt lirisë.
Every step toward education is a step toward one's freedom.[85]

Rrënjët e arsimit janë të hidhura por frutet i ka të ëmbëla.
The roots of education are bitter, but its fruit are sweet.

Jeto sikur do vdesësh nesër, mëso sikur do jetosh përgjithmonë.
Live as if you will die tomorrow, learn as if you will live forever.

Nuk është turp kur nuk di, por kur nuk dëshiron të mësosh.
There is no shame in not knowing; the shame is in not wanting to learn.

Edhe atij që ka dije mbi të gjithë, i duhet të mësoj.
Even he who is the most knowledgeable of men needs to study and learn.

---

[85] Education here is also translated as civility.

Ai që di më së shumti flet më së paku.
He who knows the most speaks the least.

Nuk mësohet plaku si do krehur mjekra.
The old man is not taught how to brush his beard.[86]

Më parë mëso veten, pastaj të tjerët.
Teach yourself first before you try teaching others.

Kush s'ka kokë, ka këmbë.
He who does not use his head uses his feet.[87]

Sa të rrosh, do mësosh.
You will learn for as long as you live.

Mësuesi më i mirë është përvoja.
Experience is the best of teachers.

Mos mëso ustanë, po merri zananë.
Instead of trying to teach the master, try learning his skills.

Ai që e ka provue din edhe me të mësue.
He who has lived an experience can also teach you about it.

Gjuha ruhet atje ku shkruhet.
Language is preserved where it is written.

---

[86] I.e. experience comes with age.
[87] I.e. he who does not plan ends up redoing his work.

Hekuri rrehet kur është i nxehtë.
Strike the iron while it is hot.[88]

Më mirë vonë se kurrë.
Better late than never.

---

[88] "Opportunity knocks but once."

Freedom, Country and Foe

Nuk ka liri pa gjak.
There is no freedom without blood.

Liria as nuk falet, as nuk blihet, por fitohet.
Freedom is neither given nor bought, it is won.

Ku ka drejtësi, aty ka liri.
Where there is justice, there is freedom.

Aty ku është drejtësia, aty është harmonia.
There is peace where there is justice.

Më mirë një ditë në liri, se njëqind vjet në robni.
Better one day free than one hundred years in slavery.[89]

Uji fle, por armiku nuk fle.
Water sleeps, but the enemy never does.

Armiku më i rrezikshëm është ai që harrohet.
The worst of enemies is the one who is forgotten.[90]

Në luftë duhen shtatë hile një trimëri.
War is seven deceptions and one courage.[91]

Më mirë të vdesësh duke luftuar, sesa të rrosh i gjunjëzuar.
Better to die fighting than to live in subjugation.

---

[89] "I'd rather die standing then live a life on my knees."
[90] "Keep your friends close and your enemies closer."
[91] I.e. as Sun Tzu wrote, "all war is deception."

Kur të jesh në dhe të huaj, dita të duket një muaj.
When in a foreign land, a day seems like a month.

Çdo zog kërkon folenë e tij.
Every bird seeks its own nest.[92]

---

[92] I.e. a person is drawn toward their home and/or country.

Hope, Health and Personal Growth

Ditë e re, nafakë e re.
A new day, a new (blessed) provision.[93]

Sharra që pret, shkëlqen edhe vetë.
The handsaw that cuts looks shiny.[94]

S'vdes i gjalli për të vdekurin.
The living do not die for the dead.[95]

I vdekuri ndjesë, i gjalli shpresë.
Condolences are for the dead, hope is for the living.[96]

Me njoftë veten është urti, me qeverisë veten, është trimni.
To know yourself is wisdom, to control yourself is courage.

Kritika është ilaç i hidhur, po ilaç ama.
A critique is a bitter medicine; and what a medicine it is!

Kurrë mos thuaj kurrë.
Never say never.

Kush duron fiton.
He who is patient wins.[97]

---

[93] "A new day, a new beginning."
[94] I.e. he who helps others also learns and benefits himself.
[95] I.e. the past is gone, don't pursue it.
[96] "Hope dies last."
[97] "All things come to those who wait."

Herë me hiri e herë pahiri, disa herë gabon edhe i miri.
At times intentionally and other times unintentionally, even the best of us fall into error.[98]

Gabimet që harrohen, përsëriten.
Mistakes forgotten are repeated.

Heshtja është flori.
Silence is gold.

Fatkeqësia më e madhe është humbja e shpresës.
The greatest of misfortunes is loss of hope.

Humbe pasurinë, hiç asgjë; humbe shëndetin, ke humbur diçka; humbe shpresën, ke humbur gjithëçka.
Lose wealth, it's nothing; lose health, you lost something; lose hope, you lost everything.

Hiq inatin, gjej rehatin.
Remove your jealousy and you will find your peace.

Koha është ajo që mbyll çdo plagë.
Time heals all wounds.

Ai që martohet herët dhe ai që ngrihet herët janë të fituar.
Winners are the ones who marry early and the ones who wake up early.[99]

---

[98] "To err is human."
[99] "Early to bed, early to rise, makes a man healthy, wealthy and wise."

Çdo pësim është mësim.
Every failure is a lesson learned.[100]

Ai që të bërtet shumë të del i mirë në fund.
He who admonishes you the most is the one who means well for you.

Ai që bëhet i urtë si delja, e hanë ujqët.
He who humbles himself like a sheep is eaten by the wolves.

Qëndro shtyllë e mos u bëj urë.
Be a pillar, not a bridge.[101]

Nuk të bën duhani burrë.
Smoking does not make you a man.

Gabimi falet një herë, e jo përherë.
A mistake is forgiven once, not every time.

Uthulla e fortë prish enën e vet.
Strong vinegar damages its own container.[102]

Kush jeton vetëm me shpresë vdes i dëshpëruar.
Whoever lives with hope alone dies a sad person.

Pas çdo dimri vjen pranvera.
After every winter comes Spring.[103]

---

[100] I.e. learn from your mistaks.
[101] I.e. stand up for your right, do not let others walk all over you or take advantage of you.
[102] I.e. he who gets angry easily often destroys his own health.
[103] "After hardship there is ease" or "Every cloud has a silver lining."

S'ka gjë pa ilaq.
There is a cure for everything.

Kush s'pyet mbetet budalla.
He who doesn't ask remains a fool.

Hidhërimi i fortë është dëm i trupit.
Immense sadness is harmful to the body.

The Power of Words and Speaking

Të flasësh pa menduar është si të zbrazësh pushkën pa e vënë në shenjë.
Speaking without thinking is like shooting without aiming.[104]

Fjala është si bleta që ka edhe mjaltin edhe thumbin.
A word is like a bee: it has the honey and the sting.[105]

Fjala ta humb, fjala ta shpëton kokën.
A word can save your life or cost your head.

Peshoje së pari fjalën pastaj nxjerre.
Weigh your words first before you say them.

Çfarë thotë gjuha del nga zemrës.
What the tongue utters comes from the heart.

Më mirë të rrëshqet këmba se sa gjuha.
It is better to have your foot slip than your tongue.

Fjala e ëmbël thyhen të fortin.
Kind words will overcome even the fiercest of men.

Fjalët e mira s'peshohen me lira.
A good word cannot be weighed with gold.

Fjala e mirë s'ka vdekje kurrë.
A good word never dies.

---

[104] I.e. one can cause great damage.
[105] I.e it can be used for good and for evil.

Fjala e mirë ilaq për zemër.
A good word is medicine for the heart.

Plagët e gjuhës janë më të këqija se plagët e pushkës.
Wounds caused by the tongue are worse than the wounds caused by the gun.

Fjala e ligë është më e rëndë se plumbi.
A wicked word hurts more than a bullet.

Fol pak e degjo shume.
Speak less and listen more.

Nuk thyen dhëmbë fjala e mbarë.
Good words do not break teeth.[106]

Fjalën, sa e ke në gojë, e ke rob tëndin, kur të del nga goja, bëhesh rob i saj.
The word, for as long as it is in your mouth, is your servant; when it leaves your mouth you become its slave.

Fjala e mirë në ditë të keqe.
Good words are for difficult days.

Heshtja eshte flori, fjala - argjend.
Words are silver, silence is gold.

Me gojë i afron, me gojë i largon shokët.
Your mouth can bring your friends closer or push them away.[107]

---

[106] I.e. no one will get angry at you if you speak kindly.
[107] I.e. use your words wisely.

Mendo dhjetë herë e fol një herë.
Think it over ten times and say it once.[108]

Fjala e tëndit të dhemb më shumë.
Hurts more the heavy word said by your own [family member].

Kur të flasësh duhet ta bësh.
When you say it you must do it.

---

[108] I.e. think well before you speak.

Money, Wealth and Influence

Pasuria nuk është lumturia.
Wealth does not equal happiness.

Pasuria dhe pozita janë mysafirë të përkohshëm.
Wealth and position are temporary guests.[109]

Më mirë të kesh mend se sa para.
Better to have brains than money.

Ai që është i pasur jep nga teprica, ai që nuk është i pasur jep nga zemra.
The rich give from their leftovers; others give from their hearts.

Nuk i thonë mik atij që e blen me të holla.
The one you buy with money is not a friend.[110]

Ai që është në fuqi bëhet se din çdo gjë.
Those in power pretend they know everything.

Ai që i mbështetet pëmes së madhe gjen hije gjithmonë.
He who leans against a big tree always finds shade.[111]

Bukuria dhe pasuria s'janë përgjithmonë.
Beauty and wealth don't last forever.

---

[109] I.e. they come and go.
[110] The person that can be bribed is not a true friend.
[111] I.e. surround yourself with reliable and stable people on whom you might later need to lean.

I pasur bëhesh me dituri jo me pasuri.
Knowledge makes you rich, not money.

Borxhi i harruar vie në ditë të shtrënguar.
Repayment of the forgotten loan is asked for when one is in great (financial) difficulty.[112]

Larg borxhit, larg rrezikut.
Out of debt, out of danger.

Parja shkon te parja.
Money goes to the money.[113]

Afër detit, afër mbretit.
Near the sea, near the king.[114]

Mos e shpenzo paranë para se ta fitosh.
Never spend money before earning it.

---

[112] I.e. do not wait to repay it.
[113] "Money makes money" or "Only the rich get richer."
[114] "The nearer the bone, the sweeter the meat."

Spouses, Love and Marriage

Dashuria e tepërt del hidhërim.
Love exceeded turns into bitterness.

Dashuria dhe kolla nuk mund të fshihen.
Love and coughing cannot be hidden.

Ai që dëshiron të shkojë përpara duhet së pari të pyes gruan e vet.
He who wants to move forward (in life) first needs to check in with his wife.

Burri për gruan është si çatia për shtëpinë.
The man for his wife is like the roof for the house.

Burri është ombrella e gruas.
A husband is his wife's umbrella.[115]

Më vështirë është të mbash dy gra se dy shtete.
It is harder to have two wives than to govern two countries.

Martesa nuk është punë që bëhet e zhbëhet.
Marriage is not a thing that is done and then undone.[116]

Edhe ai që u martua, edhe ai që nuk u martua, të dy palet pishman u bënë.
The one who got married and the one who didn't both are regretful.

---

[115] I.e. he protects her no matter what.
[116] I.e. it is a lifetime commitment.

Animals

Kush nuk i bën shërbim kalit, bën udhën në këmbë.
He who does not take care of his horse will have to travel on his feet.

Qeni që rri gjatë në hekura, nuk njeh as të zotin.
A dog that is chained for too long does not even recognize his master.

Qeni që leh nuk han.
The dog that barks doesn't bite.[117]

Barrën e kalit mos ia ngarko gomarit.
Do not put the load of a horse on a donkey.[118]

Pula bën venë e kakaris sa zgjon një mëhallë, pela bën mushkën dhe nuk ndihet fare.
The hen lays an egg and the whole neighborhood hears about it, while the mare gives birth to a foal and no one hears of it.[119]

---

[117] "Talkers are not doers."
[118] I. e. assign to people only what they can bear.
[119] I.e. some do a little but make sure everyone knows about it, others do a lot more but choose to remain quiet as to avoid public attention.

Social Good and Evil

Mirësia shpërblehet me mirësi.
Goodness is rewarded with goodness.[120]

Njeriu i lajmëruar është gjysmë i shpëtuar.
A person informed is half-saved.[121]

Shpreso për të mirën, prëgatitu për të keqën.
Hope for the best, but prepare for the worst.

Llafet janë pa bereqet.
There is no blessing in idle talk.

Urrejtja dëmton shëndetin.
Hatred harms your health.

E keqja bëhet shpejt, e mira vjen ngadalë.
Bad things happen swiftly, good things come slowly.

Gënjeshtra është nëna e të gjitha të kqijave.
Lying is the mother of all evils.

Gënjeshtra i ka këmbët e shkurtra.
A lie has short legs.[122]

Krenaria është një hap para rënies.
Pride comes right before one's downfall.

---

[120] *Mirësia* is also translated as kindness.
[121] I.e. since he knows the danger he can protect himself.
[122] I.e. it is short lived.

Mos hidh kripë në plagë.
Don't pour salt into the wound.[123]

Dëm i njërit, fitim i tjetrit.
One's detriment is the other's fortune.[124]

Mirëmëngjesi, interesi.
One greets only when in need of something.[125]

Çka ta bën goja s'ta bën armiku.
What your mouth can do to you not even your enemy will do.

Ai që ecën me krye përpjetë, bie në gropë.
He who walks with his head high will [eventually] fall into a pit.[126]

S'ka mal pa dru të shtrembër.
There is no forest with no crooked trees.[127]

Gurit të rrokullisur dhe të dehurit mos i del përpara.
Never get in the way of a rolling stone or a drunkard.

Ai që do të zihet, zihet edhe me macen.
He who wants to start a fight will fight even with a cat.

---

[123] "Don't pour vinegar into the wounds."
[124] "One man's loss is another man's gain."
[125] "Dogs wag their tails not so much in love to you as to your bread."
[126] I.e. pride and arrogance will find their match.
[127] I.e. there will always be crooked people.

Kush ha hudhra i vie era gojës.
He who has eaten garlic will emit its smell.[128]

Besnik bëhu, e bese mos zjn.
Be trustworthy, but not trusting.

Ai që di të vjedhë, di edhe të fshijë gjurmët.
He who knows how to steal also knows how to cover his tracks.

Njeriu i lig s'bëhet mik.
Do not befriend a wicked person.

Ujku do mjegull.
A wolf needs haze.[129]

Delen që ndahet nga tufa e ha ujku.
The sheep that strays is eaten by the wolf.

Tek i ligu ka pjesë shejtani.
In the wicked person Satan has a share.[130]

---

[128] I.e. if one has committed an evil act it will soon become obvious to all.
[129] I.e. he needs confusion or haze before attacking his prey.
[130] I.e. he is half human, half devil.

Good Qualities, Justice and Leadership

Njeriun e bëjnë të përjetshëm veprat e tij.
A person is made immortal by his (good) deeds.

Më mirë një luan në krye të gomerëve, se sa një gomar në krye te luanëve.
Better a lion in charge of a drove of donkeys than a donkey in charge of a pride of lions.

Kurrë mos e vlerëso njeriu nga pamja e jashtme.
Never judge a person by his appearance.[131]

E drejta dhe kandari s'kanë hatër.
There are no favors in matters of justice and matters of the scale.

Kush niset herët, arrin me kohë.
Whoever leaves early arrives on time.[132]

I drejti gjithmonë fiton.
The just person always triumphs.

---

[131] "Never judge a book by its cover."
[132] I.e. do not procrastinate.

Miscellanious

Çdo fillim ka një mbarim.
Every beginning has an end.

Më mirë pak se hiq.
A little is better than nothing.[133]

Këmbët hjekin për faj të kokës budallaqe.
The feet will suffer because of a dumb head.

Dokja të mashtron.
Appearances can be deceiving.

Kush nuk kursen të paktat, humb të shumtat.
He who is not frugal with small amounts will (eventually) lose the large amount.

Çorba e lirë t'i djeg buzët.
The cheap stew will burn your lips.[134]

Hyp se të vrava, zbrit se të vrava.
Climb or get shot, descend or get shot.[135]

I dehuri gjithnjë betohet se nuk është i pirë.
The drunkard always swears he is not drunk.

Larg syrit, larg zemrës.
What is far from the eye is far from the heart.[136]

---

[133] "Half a loaf is better than none."
[134] Cheap goods will cost you more in the long run.
[135] I.e. to be between a rock and a hard place.
[136] "Out of sight, out of mind."

Dasma e shokëve dhe lufta e huaj janë të lehta.
The weddings of friends and the wars of others are easy.[137]

Çka të hedhësh në det, e gjen në kripë.
What you throw in the sea you will find in your salt.[138]

Budallën mos e vet se t'kallxon vetë.
Don't ask a fool who he is, because he will tell you on his own.

I marri kur hesht, s'është i marrë.
A fool, when silent, is not a fool.

Kush luan me zjarr digjet.
He who plays with fire gets burned.

Ku ka tym, ka zjarr.
Where there is smoke, there is fire.

Mos i shti të gjithë në një thes.
Do not throw all in the same sack.[139]

Kur të vijnë mendtë hupin dhenët.
By the time he comes to his senses, the sheep are gone (i.e. stolen).[140]

---

[137] I.e. because those are matters that do not involve or concern you.
[138] "Never spit in a well as one day you might have to drink from it."
[139] "Different strokes for different folks."
[140] "To lock the stable door after the horse is stolen."

Appendix *A*:
The Albanian Alphabet & Transliteration Chart

Letters	Read as	Pronounce	Albanian Examples	English equivalent
A	a	a	a	afër	f<u>a</u>r
B	b	bë	b	bukë	<u>b</u>at
C	c	cë	ts	ceremoni| i<u>ts</u>y
Ç	ç	ë	tʃ	çelës	<u>ch</u>at
D	d	dë	d	dasëm	<u>d</u>oor
Dh	dh	dhë	ð	dhelpër	<u>th</u>ere
E	e	e	e	emër	<u>e</u>nter
Ë	ë	ë	ə	ëmbël	<u>a</u>round
F	f	fë	f	fletë	<u>f</u>ly
G	g	gë	g	gurë	<u>g</u>um
Gj	gj	gjë	ɟ	gjeneral| <u>j</u>oin
H	h	hë	h	hap	<u>h</u>at
I	i	i	i	ilaç	s<u>ea</u>

J	j	jë	j	javë	yawn
K	k	kë	k	këmishë	kite
L	l	lë	l	lopë	leave
Ll	ll	llë	ł or l	llampë	mill
M	m	më	m	mal	man
N	n	në	n	nënë	no
Nj	nj	një	ɲ	njeri	onion
O	o	o	o	orë	open
P	p	pë	p	parti	pen
Q	q	që	q	qumësht	mature
R	r	rë	ɾ	raport	red
Rr	rr	rrë	r (rolled)	rrjesht	borrow
S	s	së	s	stacion	stop
Sh	sh	shë	ʃ	shtëpi	shop
T	t	të	t	televizion	tree
Th	th	thë	θ	thupër	thin
U	u	u	u	urë	food
V	v	vë	v	vezë	vest

X	x	xë	dz	xixë	ad_ze_
Xh	xh	xhë	dʒ	xhaxha	_J_upiter
Y	y	y	y	yll	n_ew_*
Z	z	z	z	zemër	_z_ebra
Zh	zh	zhë	ʒ	zhurmë	plea_s_ure

*No English equivalent found. Equivalent to *mon_sieu_r* in French.

Appendix *B*:
Glossary of Terms

English	Albanian
Albania	Shqipëria
Albanian (lang.)	shqip
bird	zog
book	libër
brother	vëlla
castle	kështjellë; kala
country	shtet/vend
daughter	vajzë
day	ditë
dictionary	fjalor
English	anglisht
earth	tokë
fall/autumn	vjeshtë
father	baba

fire	zjarr
flower	lule
forest	pyll
game	lojë
hello	tungjatjeta
history	histori
hour	orë
house	shtëpi
hot	nxehtë
husband	bashkëshort
lake	liqen
language	gjuhë
library	bibliotekë
moon	hënë
no	jo
office	zyrë
people	njerëz; popull
rain	shi
foot	këmbë

river	lumë
sea	det
sky	qiell
snow	borë
son	djalë; bir
spring	pranverë
summer	verë
star	yll
time	kohë
tree	pemë
wife	bashkëshorte
winter	dimër
yes	po
God	Zot

Appendix C:
Timeline of Albanian History[141]

334-323 BCE – Alexander the Great controls the region

168 BCE – Romans conquer Illyria

547 CE – First Slavic invasions begin

850s – Kosova (then Dardania) is absorbed by the Bulgarian Empire

700-800s – Slavic tribes invade Illyrian lands and start settling the region

1018 – The region becomes part of Byzantium

1184-1196 – Under Stefan Nemanja I, the Serbs expand from Rascia into eastern Kosova

1208-1216 – With the conquest of Prizren under Stefan Nemanja II most of Kosova falls under Serbian rule

1219-1300s – The period under the rule of the Serbian

---

[141] For more information on the timeline, see BBC News Timeline: Kosovo; BBC NEWS Timeline: Albania; *The Balkan Wars* by A. Gerolymatos; *Kosovo* by J. Meritus; *Kosovo in a Nutshell* by R. Elsie; and Kosova: A Timeline by K. Beig.

principality of Rascia witnesses the building of Serbian Orthodox churches and monasteries across Kosova and the region

1345-1371 – Ottomans appear in the Balkans

1389 – The armies of the Balkans (Serbs, Albanians, Bosnians, and others) under King Lazar are defeated at the Battle of Kosova (the Field of Blackbirds) by the Ottoman armies under the rule of Sultan Murad I

1396-1423 – Elements of Ottoman administration are set up in various parts of Kosova

1443 – Skanderbeg rebels and fights back the Ottomans

1448 – Second Battle of Kosova consolidates Ottoman rule in the Balkans

1453 – Sultan Mehmet Fatih conquers Constantinople (and names it *Istanbul*); Albania and Kosova become province of the Ottoman Empire

1467 – The Albanian Kingdom comes under direct control of the Ottomans, enjoying internal autonomy

1521 – Sultan Suleiman the Magnificent conquers Belgrade (the capital of Serbia)

1600-1700 – The majority of Albanians willingly convert to Islam because of the great Ottoman example, and some in order to be exempt from paying the *jizya* (per capita tax on non-Muslims of a Muslim state)

1689 – A Habsburg army conquers Kosova but are shortly forced to withdraw

1737 – Habsburg forces capture Prishtina but weeks later abandon Kosova

1785 – Kara Mahmud Pasha Bushatliu of Shkodra captures most of Kosova

1877-1878 – The Ottomans lose foothold in Serbia, Montenegro and Bulgaria because of the Russo-Ottoman war; Serbs expel some 50,000 Muslims to Kosova from the Sanjak of Niš

1878 – Serbs occupy parts of Kosova; Treaty of San Stefano give parts of Kosova to Serbia and Montenegro; The League of Prizren (made up of mostly Muslim delegates) meets in Prizren in response to the treaty; The League also demands autonomy of Albania within Ottoman rule

1880 – The League of Prizren controls most of Kosova

1881 – Ottoman forces disperse the League and reclaim most of Kosova

1903-1912 – Albanian uprisings against the Young Turks take place in various cities of Kosova and beyond

1912 – The First Balkan War; Albania declares independence from the Ottomans; Serbs occupy Kosova

1913 – Kosova becomes part of the Kingdom of Serbia; estimated that 25,000 Albanians killed during Serb invasion

1915 – Bulgarian troops invade parts of Kosova

1918 – Kosova is retaken by Serbs

1919 – Serbs pillage throughout Kosova and kill over 6,000 Kosovar Albanians

1928 – The number of Serb colonists introduced to Kosova by the Serbian government is raised from 24 percent in 1919 to 38 percent

1929 – The Kingdom of the Serbs, Croats of Slovenes now is called Yugoslavia; Kosova is brought under Yugoslav rule

1933-1935 – The Yugoslav government begins the deportation of the Muslim Albanian communities to Turkey; the Yugoslav government begins confiscation of lands belonging to the local Kosovar Albanians

1937 – Serbian Vaso Čubrilović writes the secret memorandum "Expulsion of Albanians," advocating for a forced removal of all Albanians from Kosova who are around 90% Muslim

1939 – Italy invades Albania; Albania rescues 100 percent of the Jewish population there during WWII

1941 – Josip Tito organizes the partisan movement in

Yugoslavia; Kosova becomes part of the Italian-controlled Albania; Enver Hoxha takes lead of the Communist Party

1943 – Germany invades Albania

1944 – Communists in Albania establish provisional government and appoint Enver Hoxha as Prime Minister

1945 – Churchill gives Kosova, Macedonia, Slovenia and Croatia to Communist Yugoslavia under the rule of Tito; Yugoslavia introduces military rule in Kosova; religious communities suffer a reign of terror

1945-1951 – Thousands of Kosovar Albanians are murdered and expelled to Turkey after being labeled as "Turks" because of their shared faith with the majority of Turkish people

1948-1950 – Yugoslav-Albanian relations fall apart; borders are sealed

1946 – Kosova is absorbed into the Yugoslav federation; Socialist People's Republic of Albania is proclaimed

1961 – Albania allies itself with China

1948 – Tito breaks with USSR

1968 – First demonstrations for independence in Kosova, during which many were arrested

1974 - The Yugoslavian constitution declares Kosova an

Autonomous Province of Yugoslavia

1980 – Yugoslav leader Tito dies; Serbs begin their campaign to retake Kosova from Albanians and make it a province of Greater Serbia

1981 – Kosovar Albanian students at the University of Prishtina begin rioting in defense of Kosovar Albanian rights; hundreds of peaceful Kosovar demonstrators are wounded and killed

1981-1989 – The Serbian campaign against Kosovar Albanians intensifies. Hundreds of students are poisoned by the food given to them at their schools

1985 – Albania's dictator, Enver Hoxha, dies

1989 – Serbian leader Slobodan Milošević rallies thousands of Serbs at the Field of Blackbirds to remind them that Serbs will never give up Kosova, "the Heart of Serbia," and that the economical and political sufferings of the Serbs in Kosova are because of the high constitutional status of the Albanians in Yugoslavia

1989-1990 – Milošević takes away Kosova's constitutional status as an autonomous province and reduces the country to an integral part of Serbia. Milošević abolishes the Assembly of Kosova and dissolves its government. Kosovar employees are fired. The campaign for the closing of all Albanian schools begins. The Albanian-speaking media is silenced; health services and other institutional funds for Albanians are usurped

1991 – The Yugoslav Federation is dissolved; the European Community (now European Uunion) establishes an Arbitration Commission to make decisions regarding recognition of its former constituents as independent countries. This Commission accepts Slovenia's and Croatia's applications, but not that of Bosnia or Kosova

1992 – Albania's Democratic Party wins elections, and Salih Berisha becomes president. In Kosova, Ibrahim Rugova, an advocate of non-violence, is elected the first president of the Republic of Kosova; unofficial referendum among ethnic Albanians in Macedonia shows overwhelming wish for their own territorial autonomy; Bosnia holds its referendum and 99 percent of the ballots come in favor of independence. However, at the time, the Serbian government was preparing for the slaughter of thousands of Bosnian Muslims

1992-1995 – Serbian extremists carry out genocide in Bosnia. In July of 1995, two years after being declared a "Safe Haven" by the UN, around 8,000 Bosnian Muslims are massacred in Srebrenica

1995 – Talks are held at Dayton, Ohio, to resolve the Balkan crisis. Bosnia is divided into a Serb and a Muslim-Croat federation

1996-97 – Hate-filled Serbian nationalist, Vojislav Šešelj, publicly advocates infecting Kosovar Albanians with the AIDS virus; the Kosova Liberation Army (KLA) emerges as a reaction to the presence of the Serbian regime throughout Kosova

1997 – Unrest in Albania brings the Socialists to power; Serbian military offensive increases tremendously in Kosova; U.S. and E.U. diplomats are repeatedly deceived by Milošević's false promises to end his campaign of ethnic cleansing

1998 – Milošević and Rugova hold talks for the first time but without any results; Serbian forces attack central Kosova, killing many Albanian civilians; international diplomacy fails; NATO allies airstrike Serbian military targets; in October, Milošević agrees to withdraw troops and allow refugees to return, and Belgrade agrees to allow 2,000 unarmed international monitors to verify compliance; envoy Christopher Hill tries to broker political settlement, but violence undermines cease-fire

1999 – In January, 45 Albanian men were killed in Racak and 24 more were killed later that month; the Western allies demand peace talks from both sides or face airstrikes; in February, both parties met in Rambouliett, France; that month Serbian forces attack KLA positions and KLA fights back; in March, Kosovar Albanian leaders sign the peace deal which gave them a "broad interim autonomy" and 28,000 NATO troops to keep the peace. The deal also requires the disbandment of the KLA, but surprisingly Serbian authorities refuse the deal, and this suspends the talks

1999 – On March 20, international peace monitors evacuate Kosova while NATO prepares to start bombardments; on the 22nd Richard Holbrooke warns Milošević of airstrikes for the last time, but Milošević still refuses to allow NATO troops in Kosova; on the 24th airstrikes against Serbian military targets begin; Serbian atrocities continue against Kosovar Albanian civilians

1999 – In April, over 600,000 Kosovar Albanians are forced to leave their homes during NATO airstrikes, their properties are looted and homes are burned; thousands of people are murdered; the Western allies refuse to arm the KLA because of the arms embargo placed on Yugoslavia; by May Serbian troops increase in Kosova and over a million Kosovar Albanians are expelled; Milošević is indicted for war crimes by the International Criminal Tribune

1999 – In June, NATO's 72-day airstrike campaign ends the Serbian occupation of Kosova; UN Security Council passes the Security Council Resolution 1244 placing Kosova under transitional UN administration (UNMIK)

2000 – Now declared a war criminal, Milošević runs again for president, but loses national elections in Serbia

2001-2002 – Because of its considerable Albanian population there, Macedonian parliament recognizes Albanian as an official language

2002 – At the Hague, Milošević's trial begins; he dies four years later at the Hague

2003 – The Socialist Party wins in Albania

2006 – In January, President Rugova dies and is succeeded by Fatmir Sejdiu; in October, Serbian voters in a referendum in Serbia approve a new constitution which declares Kosova an integral part of Serbia, and Kosovar Albanians boycott the ballot

2007 – In February, the UN envoy Martti Ahtisaari unveils the plan to set Kosova on its road to independence, and Serbia and Russia reject it

2008 – On February 17, Kosova declares independence, but Serbia rejects it, calling it illegal under international law; in April, Kosova's parliament adopts new constitution; in December, the E.U. mission (Eulex) takes over police, justice and customs services from the UN in Kosova; Macedonia recognizes Kosova's independence

2009 – Albania joins NATO

2010 – In response to Serbian claims, the UN International Court of Justice rules that Kosova's declaration of independence was not illegal under any international law

2012 – Period of Kosova's international supervision of independence ends

2015-2017 – Middle East refugees appear in the Balkans

making their way to northern Europe

ACKNOWLEDGMENTS

First of all, I praise and thank the All-Merciful Creator for enabling me to bring forth these great reminders from the treasures of Albanian culture. Secondly, there are numerous family members, friends and mentors I wish to thank and acknowledge for their tremendous support. Countless thanks to my wife for her patience with me, and for going over my work. Heart-felt thanks to Ilir Bekteshi, Rick Williams, Brandon Mayfield, and Stella Williams for proofreading this collection of sayings. Also, my deep appreciations go to Burhan Al-Din Fili, Linda Barnes, Didmar Faja, Paul Fattig, Abdullah Alkadi, Joel Hayward, and Amber Haque for their invaluable support and friendship. Special thanks also to Hon. Joe & Shirley DioGuardi, Masud and Salma Ahmad, Maqsood & Eloisa Chaudhary, Mike and Linda Tresemer, Rania Ayoub, Judith Jensen, Brian Carter, Bruce Stanbridge, Philip Randall, Imran Maqbool, Lori & David Sours, Amy Lepon, Bruce Beaton, Ahmed Al-Baloushi, Mohammad Al-Rashdi, Ali and Aziz Govori, and the following families: Brady and Wright, Offenbacher, Bresa, Jaffar, Maralusha, Wood, Yavuz, Acar, Obaidi, Mirza, Rockholt & Manlulu, Petersen, Sumariwallah, Gashi, and many more.

ABOUT THE AUTHOR

Flamur Vehapi is a poet, literary translator, academic and student of peace and conflict resolution. He was born in Kosova and later exiled by the Serbian regime in the late 1990s. After moving to the United States, he received his AA and BS in psychology with a minor in history. In 2013, he received his MA in conflict resolution from Portland State University. Flamur has taught social sciences at Rogue Community College and Southern Oregon University, and most recently he has taught in the Middle East. His works include *The Alchemy of Mind* and *A Cup with Rumi*, both collections of spiritual poems. His latest book is *Peace and Conflict Resolution in Islam*. Flamur and his family currently live in Oregon.

REFERENCES AND SUGGESTED READINGS

Cordry, Harold. *The Multicultural Dictionary Of Proverbs*. 1st ed. Jefferson, NC, McFarland & Company, 1997.

Durham, Edith. *High Albania*. Boston, Beacon Press, 1985.

Elsie, Robert. *A Dictionary Of Albanian Religion, Mythology And Folk Culture*. New York: NYU Press, 2001.

Hasan, Hamdi. *Makedonya Ve Kosova Türklerince Kullanılan Atasözleri Ve Deyimler*. 1st ed. Ankara, Türk Dil Kurumu, 1997.

Inalcık, Halil. *The Ottoman Empire: The Classical Age 1300-1600*. London, Phoenix, 2001.

Itzkowitz, Norman. *Ottoman Empire And Islamic Tradition*. Chicago, University Of Chicago Press, 1980.

Jacques, Edwin. *The Albanians: An Ethnic History From Prehistoric Times To The Present*. Jefferson, Mcfarland, 2009.

Janaqi, Alba (Ed). *Fjalë Të Urta Krahinore*. Tiranë, Reklama,

2011.

Judah, Tim. *Kosovo*. Oxford, Oxford University Press, 2008.

Kaplan, Robert. *Balkan Ghosts: A Journey Through History*. NY, Picador, 2005.

Kasmi, Kolë. *Goja e popullit*. Tiranë, N.p., 1943.

Kolea, Sotir. *Një Tufë*. Tiranë, N.p., 1944.

Malcolm, Noel. *Agents of Empire*. NY, Oxford University Press, 2015.

___. *Kosovo: A Short History*. NY, Harper Perennial, 1998.

Sako, Zihni. *Historia e Letërsisë Shqipe I*, Tiranë, N.p., 1959.

Sarner, Harvey. *Rescue In Albania*. Cathedral City, CA., Brunswick Press, 1997.

Shuteriqi, Dhimitër. *Shkrimet Shqipe Në Vitet 1332-1850*. Tiranë, Mihal Duri, 1979.

Spahiu, Agim. *Fjalët e Urta në FGJSSH*. Vrojtime Leksikografike, N.p., 2008, from http://www.shkenca.org/pdf/gjuhe/fjalet_e_urta.pdf

Wilkes, John. *The Illyrians.* Oxford (UK), Blackwell, 2000.

Yurtbasi, Metin. *A Dictionary Of Turkish Proverbs.* 1st ed. Ankara, Turkish Daily News, 1993.

ABOUT THE TYPE

The text of this book was set in Garamond. Garamond is a group of many old-style serif typefaces, named for sixteenth-century Parisian engraver Claude Garamond. Garamond-style typefaces are popular and often used, particularly for printing body text and books.

NOTES

NOTES

Printed in Dunstable, United Kingdom